Immigration Is the Essence of Democracy

Immigration Is the Essence of Democracy

Poems by

Peter Waldor

© 2025 Peter Waldor. All rights reserved.
This material may not be reproduced in any form, published,
reprinted, recorded, performed, broadcast,
rewritten or redistributed without
the explicit permission of Peter Waldor.
All such actions are strictly prohibited by law.

Cover design by Shay Culligan
Cover image by Nicole Herrero on Unsplash
Author photo by Gabriel Waldor

ISBN: 978-1-63980-819-9

Kelsay Books
502 South 1040 East, A-119
American Fork, Utah 84003
Kelsaybooks.com

for Gabriel, Nathaniel and Jacob

Other Books by Peter Waldor

Door to a Noisy Room
The Wilderness Poetry of Wu Xing
Who Touches Everything
The Unattended Harp
State of the Union
Gate Posts with No Gate
Nice Dumpling
Owl Gulch Elegies
Unmade Friend
Something About the Way
The Way 2
Midwife vs Obstetrician
Hats Off
Seven Quilts (essays)
Snowy Saplings
Understandings and Misunderstandings
At the Next Table
Time Can't Tell It's Being Told
Beginning Polyamory
Fairy Slippers
wellwhadayasay?
Turnstiles
14 Meditation Prompts and a Treatise on Noble Silence
The Third Way
You Alone Know
Tapadawhirld
Intermediate Polyamory
The Way Fourth
One Can NEVER Predict the Past

Contents

Immigration Is the Essence of Democracy	15
Slim or Solomon	16
Hot Off the Press	19
Late-Stage Capitalism	20
The Great Drum	22
In the Irving Penn portrait	24
Advice	26
Romantic Advice to My Children	28
All Groves Are Sacred	29
Teenagers	31
Careful When Swimming	33
Kind Server	35
Green Hoodie	37
Is It Ego?	38
Half a Muffler	39
Mille Fiore	40
Lessons	41
Parent and Child	42
Sliding Rock	43
Art and Pharmaceuticals	44
Bless the Lonely Man, Bless Them All	46
Eddie	49
AGI and UBI	50
At what point	51
Drag or Cross-Dress?	52

X

The Twelve Commandments of Peaceful Nations	57
The Great International No Secrets Agreement	59

Assholes	60
Il Duce	61
Point and Clench	62
But Not Heavy	64
Das Kapital	66
Great Table	67
Two Parents' Views of Hypocritical Socialism	68
I Can't Say Where	69
Days Inn	70

X

Peeled Orange	75
Man in Black	76
Gentle Giant	77
Duned Up	78
Maw	79
An Elder	80
Blessings	81
Baby Taj	84
Guru	86
Ithaca	87
Cocktail	88
Two Fifties	90
A Dear Friend	91
Chunky	92
Schadenfreude	94
Erhu	96
Two Bills	97
Howl's End	99

Pablo Picasso	104
Sunday Morning	106
Grant Street	108
Joan as Policewoman Prepares to Sing	109
Immigration Is the Essence of Democracy	110

Anyone should be able to knock on any door

Immigration Is the Essence of Democracy

A woman sits on the Columbus Ave sidewalk,
straight legs angled out like the banks
of a river delta, her small pack propped
behind her back, full of everything
she kept from Port-Au-Prince. She doesn't
seem to mind the dirty paving stones.
She has a large sketch pad between her legs
and she sketches you as you step around her.
You are trying not to look at her and yet looking.
She sees you and understands you
better than anyone.

Slim or Solomon

poured hot water,
sweetened and spiced, over fresh
mint jammed in the tops of our tea
glasses, my glass tinted green, my love's
yellow. Slim could have kept the slender
pewter spout an inch above the glasses
but he slowly lifted the ornate teapot
higher, almost to the height of his
forehead so the hot water fell in
a hot waterfall, into our glasses,
frothy, milky, steamy, slender,
and delicate, purely for our pleasure,
for our glittering pleasure.
Solomon speaks Arabic, his
Algerian dialect, French, Italian, and
Spanish, and don't forget English,
the language he spoke with us, though
he said *shukran,* a word he knew
we would know when we said goodbye.
He lifted the pot higher and higher
like a magician and I wondered
if the bead of water got slenderer as
it elevated, as it stretched; and the
miraculous way it fell into our narrow
topped glasses and not our laps
reminded me of Dumbo, the poor
circus elephant, diving from
the high platform, through the flames,
and landing in the small tub of water;

but this waterfall didn't seem
unhappy to obey the lawlessness
of physics as it crashed through the mint
barricade into our narrow glasses.
Before we said goodbye we said
we hoped we'd meet again.
He told us people like to call him Slim
so I called him Slim but I could see
my love with the yellow glass
grimace when I did so as if I
had taken a liberty, and with
one so esteemed as Solomon,
at that. I say he is just as esteemed
as Slim; or I don't say. I thought.
Some restaurants are full and
should be empty and some are
empty that should be full.
Solomon's was nearly empty,
just us and a couple others
enjoying the great Moroccan
Tajines, while every other place
on the street was overflowing
with people waiting to eat mushy
overcooked fish drowned in
butter and Italian spices.
Slim didn't seem alarmed by
the emptiness and he had time
to chat and pour. Two handsome boys
peered in, then entered, clearly stoned.

Slim hugged them and said be careful
and told us the boys were regulars
at his crepe place around the corner
on Columbus. I guess crepes are
good for the munchies. The water
hitting the mint sounded like dried
peas spilling from a sack onto an
empty storeroom floor. In Judaism
there is something called an eternal
flame. Solomon's waterfall is also
eternal. Can you see it? Hear it?
Smell its mint ending? Taste?
It's all around us.

Hot Off the Press

The kind young Gabonese man
at the register in the corner
market offered to squeeze
me a fresh container when
I asked him if the orange
juice was squeezed today.
And when he did the squeeze
in front of me I couldn't think
of a clichéd expression to
honor the job, like *strike
while the iron is hot,*
so I debated a split second and said
the best thing that came to mind,
hot off the press, and he laughed
lightly which he wouldn't have done
had there been an apt expression,
and now it's time for a new saying—
*there is no good deed greater than
making a stranger laugh,* especially
a bare acquaintance, at the beginning
of his long work day, and far
from the village of his birth.

Late-Stage Capitalism

Its tragedy is expressed
through comedy
in an SFO bathroom
where the sinks have
sensors so the hands
need not make any
contact but the
sensor failure rate
is over 50% and I saw
Groucho Marx go down
the row of ten sinks
and hold his palms
in the proper sensing
zone, palms out as if
for a fortuneteller
or his mother Rae's
inspection, and the first
nine sinks did not
trigger the plumbing
network at all
and then the tenth
engaged but only
briefly either due to
partial malfunction
or recalibration to
mitigate the effects
of our perpetual
drought. There was
only one towel

dispenser to
accommodate
the ten sinks and
Groucho's hands,
of course,
did not engage its
sensor either
and so he wiped
the little splash
he did get on the
back of his baggy
black satin trousers.
I could see his
palm prints on
both his buttocks.
I laughed and cried.

The Great Drum

My child is quite culturish-vulturish
because they love all cultures
and worked as a shepherd
at a vulture sanctuary, fattening
sheep and slaughtering them
for the endangered vultures
and when they were taking far
too long to absorb the Penn
comma Irving photography
exhibit I asked the young guard
who was tall, bearded,
and strapping, to tap my
child's shoulder and say
sir the museum would like
you to exit pronto, and I know
the guard was thinking
no one ever asked him
to do something that
outrageous and he could
get fired if he did it and it
violated the international
conventions of the League
of Museum Guards, but as
he was ruminating and I was
urging him on, my child happened
to pause in front of him
and he seized the opportunity
without any further wise
reflection and tapped their

shoulder and said *sir it's
time for you to go,*
and he let out a deep laugh,
five big *huh*s—*huh, huh, huh
huh, huh*—and I thought
of a giant drum, the size
of a round card table
and a large man beating
the drum with a heavy mallet,
furiously, five times, each
beat one of the five *huh*s,
and I was the sheepskin
taut on top, five times
the mallet beat me—*huh,
huh, huh, huh, huh*. Beaten
by laughter, we walked away,
arm in arm, limping from laughter,
out of the garden, or was it
into the garden. I only
turned back to wink at
my brother the guard, who
was winking at me.

In the Irving Penn portrait

of Doug, the Hell's Angel,
Doug is slightly plump, zaftig,
with glistening, fugazi heavy,
lazily brushed hair, and he
recalls what a friend told me
of his brother who was also
an angel from hell and named
Doug and lived at the same
time and place when and
where Penn made the photo.
The photo shared a resemblance
to what I imagine a younger
version of my friend's brother
would look like, and my friend's
brother Doug was not a
run of the mill angel but in
the upper ranks, and his nickname
was Dirty Doug because he
was their *bomber,* an
enforcer who used explosive
devices, and so when Penn's
advance woman contacted
the Angels, it would be no
stretch to imagine her
making her way to my
friend's brother Doug
who eventually renounced
violence and took up
African drumming. I don't

understand my friend's
lack of curiosity about my
theory; perhaps it's his
diffidence related to all
family and childhood
matters due to the difficulty
and trauma of those years,
or a general lack of curiosity
probably a result of his
already knowing everything
about everything and so
there being no need to bother.
After all, he's spent his life
trying to remake the world
so there are no bombers,
just drummers shaking
the earth so anyone can
love anyone without fear.

Advice

Teenagers are people and people
hate advice, at least good advice,
but perhaps my teen friends
will allow me to repeat a story
they told me, and draw the
opposite conclusion. They were
visiting a dear friend of theirs
in a special place, a hot spring
in a desert. Their friend, kind, funny,
brilliant. As a ten-year-old he knit
a wool facsimile of a chainmail
hat and gator. Another of
his many wonders, he played
chess by using USPS handwritten
correspondence. Each player
wrote their next move following
long philosophical explorations.
My friends noticed he was
starting to have flashes of quiet
brooding, alienation, just as his
father had been overcome,
dragging his graying beard around
like the train of a dress, ignoring
his children and partner. I know they
are frightened for him, for they love
him and they are frightened
for themselves, for they were sure
they will be the most different
people in the world from their

parents. My opposite conclusion
to this story is that their friend will
overcome his brooding and they
will all be as different as they
need to be. I know them all
and have full confidence in them.

Romantic Advice to My Children

You may be inclined to think that
the *other* knows everything
and you know nothing, that
you're the young student and
they're the aged master, blind,
with wispy goatee, and the
truth is they may know a lot,
but don't forget you know
more than a little, and if your
heart is beating so loud even
a non-vampire can hear it,
don't forget you're too young
to have a heart attack, and if
the suffering may seem like
too much to bear, think of it
as a kind of dark pleasure that
can almost be enjoyed. I know
you're all smart enough to
ignore my advice, but consider
this at least.

All Groves Are Sacred

Kids these days can't just
climb a tree, they have to break
into a sacred grove and not just
climb one tree but swing from tree
to tree like flying squirrels, and my
three boys were swinging just fine
when one fell and we thought he
broke his wrist, but after a few
minutes icing from a bag contributed
by an Italian restaurant he was
restored enough to keep up with his
brothers. All day they debated if
a structure was brutalist, ecobrutalist,
neolithic brutalist, ecolithic neo-
brutalist, or, god forbid, not
brutalist at all, which, sadly, is mostly
the case in our city now, and I felt
no impatience with their lengthy debate.
On our walk, before the tree swinging,
they found a long extension cord,
the plug missing on one end,
the butt covered with black tape.
It was about fifty-feet long and one
of them whipped it so it made humps
like a sea dragon breaking the water.
Strangers had to dance occasionally
to avoid the darting beast and I could see
others looking on with fright and since I
was what people call an *elder* I knew

it was my role to tell them to stop,
but I was a strangely silent elder.
And then, though the boys
seemed eternally wedded to that cord
and all the beauty and performance
they could whip out of it, they abruptly
dropped it in the middle of a large
and busy sidewalk and I sheepishly
moved it to the less traveled side,
sheepish for fear of the looks from
people walking by and sheepish
from the boys' looks. They left
the cord with no cord-leaving ceremony,
with no thought for who the next
ones would be to pick up the thread
and make something out of nothing.
Then they slid down a long and
perilously steep railing, all three at once.
My gut knotted at their speed.
Then they ate bread for lunch, bread alone.
They tore the loaf roughly, no knife.
They toasted with the bread as if
it were wine. One boy said
To each according to his needs,
another *From each according to his*
abilities and the last one—*To and from*
everyone, art in all its future unknown forms.
And it was only the middle of the day.

Teenagers

Big Wind but
not so big
to knock a girl
down, a girl who
elegantly steps
in front of her
pack of friends,
and falls
back into them
pretending the
big wind had
knocked her
backwards
and the three
or four friends
all reach their
hands out to
catch her.
They think
it's funny
but none
laugh because
this is the sort
of shit she
pulls and they
don't want to
encourage her.
After all they
want to make it

to the 7-11 and
back during
their ten minutes
of freedom.

Careful When Swimming

As much as I hate the idea of City Lights Bookshop
curating a time, place, and movement that never
existed in the way anybody claims,
when the man in front of me checked out with
the volume of Shelley's *Complete Poetry and Prose*,
thick as two bibles and the very OED definition
of boring and impenetrable, the cashier,
who is spearheading a unionization
effort despite the shop being perpetually
on the brink, told the clean-cut man who
I wondered about (clean-cut and Shelley?)
to *please be careful when swimming,*
and I loved, not the idea, but the living, breathing
place of City Lights. The Shelley man showed no
reaction, as if he didn't even hear, and left
with the tome and its randomly placed bookmark.
And then it was my turn. I was just buying
a postcard picture of the shop, because
I am more interested in the pictorial rather than
the literary tradition. I asked the clerk if she was
referring to Shelley's drowning and she said
of course, cheerily bored by my question,
and then she told me about all the tragic
early deaths among the romantics, Keats at 23,
by consumption, Byron, at 36, at war,
Shelley at 39, drowning. I was too shy to ask
her about Wordsworth, dead at 90, and famous.
Would she say he was not a true romantic?
And what about Christopher Smart, dead at 49

in debtor's prison, two years before Coleridge was born?
Coleridge, whose ink ran out long before his death at 61.
Was Smart the first and last true romantic?
We are in debt to him now more than any of the others.
For he is docile and can learn certain things (his cat Joffrey).
For he can spraggle upon waggle at the word of command.
Will the already heavy *Complete Shelley* weigh more
after it fills with all its future underlinings?

Kind Server

Since I had no
staring privileges
I didn't want to risk
that beautiful word
opprobrium so I
looked only glancingly,
furtively, at your
nails which seemed
to have a little
dirt tucked
under the end
of each one,
ten black crescents,
the translucent
keratin somehow
darkening the dirt,
even idealizing it,
and you, in your
natty black suit,
moving your hands
with economy,
yielded only one
personal detail—
that your car
died that morning,
and then I saw too
much, as I do, and
saw that it was not
dirt but nail polish,

black, deftly done
to look like dirt
at the edges of each
sculpted nail.
I'll never think of
polish the same way,
or art, or dirt, which
someone once called
the ecstatic skin of
the earth. The biblical
phrase shouldn't
be dust to dust but
dirt to dirt and your
small rebellion,
if that's what it is,
teaches me the great
beauty of the small
rebellion.

Green Hoodie

Dapper old man scampers along
faster than a sparrow and chirps
sweet hellos to all as he passes.
His neat green hoodie said
Gang Green, a nickname,
I believe, for a big-ten football
team. I am not sensitive
but I imagine a sensitive person
shaking the man and chastising
you fool what happens if someone
who suffered from gangrene
or one of their loved ones or
family or friends or tangential
acquaintances or even strangers
they've heard about suffered or
died from gangrene and they
saw your hoodie with its facile pun?
What happens if they crumpled in despair?
Shame on you, you cad.
Shame on humanity.
But I just chirped hello. In fact
I was first to chirp.

Is It Ego?

The Tea Hut is shut
but a man lets himself in
and leans against the counter,
with his thoughts, and I move
on in my thoughts, until
another man with a gleaming
canister of pesticide
approaches, and the man
alone with his thoughts
lets the other in.
The two confer quietly,
gently, and I project,
with sadness, for the soon-
to-be-dead insects.
I'm leaning, writing,
against the top
of a garbage can. I have
never been this close to
someone else's garbage.
I like it. Now I find a note
in my pocket that says
Is it ego? I was apparently
anxious enough to write
that down, so I'd be sure
to remember to ask,
not sure who or when
or where, or if it was
I that needed to
answer the question.

Half a Muffler

He had a nice hoodie
but wasn't smart enough
to raise the hood
when it got cold.
He was fed up, with me,
maybe the world,
and walked away,
maybe that was smart
enough, and the wind
was at his back, and it
blew the hood up his
beautiful pale neck
so it was half a muffler.
I pray that little extra
warmth will be the
difference for him.

Mille Fiore

Now that you're old enough
to seek more names,
can I make a humble suggestion
for somewhere in the middle,
between your first and last,
add *mille fiore,* it means
a thousand flowers, and it's
also a decorative glassblowing
technique that echoes the idea
of many flowers. You flower lover
and glassblower! And now
that I am old enough to
dream of getting rid of the
few names I have, I implore
you to leave my discarded
names in the sewer I'll
toss them in. God forbid
you should pick one up.
Look how that turned out
for humanity so far.

Lessons

My child told me
that many years
ago I told him if
I had an opportunity
to assassinate Hitler
I would not, as I was
and am a pacifist.
What was I thinking
then, what am I
thinking now? Does
the child have to
remember everything?

Parent and Child

And here I am arguing
with my child, not arguing,
or maybe I am but
they're just laughing
when I tell them I am not
only bisexual but pansexual,
and panner than Pan
at that, and, by the way
I'm not a man but
post-gendered, free.
They're just laughing,
not even bothering
to argue, they're so
sure I'm full of shit.

Sliding Rock

Before I could stop my son
he slides a six-hundred-year-
old carved stone out of an
Incan wall. There is a smooth
sliding sound of one rock
moving against another,
for the first time in six-hundred
years, or I should say, the second
time, the first was the original
mason and the second,
my son, both slides executed
with exquisite, gentle care.
Was my son also the mason,
long ago? I'll do what I can
to try not to stop him from
living his own life. He slides
the stone back in and smiles.
And no one who sees
the wall will ever know
how that one stone slid
into place, twice.

Art and Pharmaceuticals

The youth group, rambling
around town after a meeting,
broke into a pharmacy and each
teenager took a bottle of pills.
They spent a few days shaking
them to ascertain timbre and tone
and a few more days to work
on their semi-improvisational
piece, and then in three lines,
each five children deep,
they walked through town,
performing, 15 rattles,
sometimes solo, like the first
frog in an early spring pond,
sometimes in sections,
sometimes altogether.
In their orchestration
they ignored drug names
and intended uses, both out of
ignorance and indifference,
but they did place erectile
enhancements in one section,
shaking rapidly in unison
with the right-hand while
the left arm was raised up,
palms either open or in fists.
The audience, that is the town
going about its business,
had no idea about the origin

of the rattles, which is often
how it is with art. And after
a few parades, the kids
threw the bottles away,
which is how it should be
with art and pharmaceuticals.

Bless the Lonely Man, Bless Them All

There are hierarchies and there aren't
hierarchies. Willie Davis, an African
American, was a certified heavy
equipment operating engineer.
Manuel Melo, Caucasian, Portuguese,
was the foreman, though I'm not sure
who answered to who. Manuel would
whistle at Willie in the giant backhoe,
and then make a rapid sweeping motion
with his left arm when Willie had dug
the trench deep enough, a sign to pull
the remaining dirt, gravel, rocks, away.
There was a flourish to the arm motion,
as if he were a bullfighter sweeping
the red velvet cape across his midsection
after the bull rushed past, but there was
no death of majestic creatures here,
just the arm in an oval alacrity,
and an abrupt ending, and I was the
low man, the summer grunt, ferrying
cement buckets and hay bales, but my
father was a successful insurance man,
so I was off to college after that summer,
and today, 45 years later, my artist friend,
Dan Collins, was trenching with his
little backhoe and I swept with my
left arm when he sunk the teeth
deep enough, and I remembered
Manuel. Was it Manuel sweeping

his arm today, not me?
Forty-five years ago I saw nothing
special about it, but today I see no
greater majesty than Manuel's small
strong arm and the way Willie calmy
spun the many levers in his cockpit,
safely moving the tons of metal
just inches from us. There are
hierarchies and there are no hierarchies,
at least over lunch, where, on hot
days, we sheltered in the shade
of one of the giant sewer pipe sections
before Willie lowered it in the earth
that afternoon. Bless them all,
everyone kind, even when they
made fun of my incompetence
at cement mixing, and Dan here
today, kind, he loves machines,
and is a friend happy to dig our trench.
He was an early performance artist
that summer I met Willie and Manuel.
He used scrim cloth and its
unique properties of light, shadow,
and transparency to plum mysteries,
and once, with little money, as a late
teenager, in a storm on the outskirts
of Paris, he found shelter for the night
in a sewer pipe that hadn't been laid
by one of Willie's French brothers

or sisters. He woke in the middle of the
night when the mists had cleared and in
the giant aperture of the pipe was the
tower of Notre Dame. He squinted and
was sure he saw Quasimodo on the belfry,
and he yelled *ahoy Quasimodo* in the
echoing pipe, until he was hoarse,
knowing no one could hear him.
Please yell with him now, *ahoy Quasimodo,
ahoy Quasimodo, ahoy Quasimodo.*
Bless the lonely man.

Eddie

knew you and I always wished
he knew me but I didn't
think it would ever happen
but today it happened, he smiled
that smile he reserved for very
few people, for me.
I hope it wasn't competitiveness
that made me yearn so
for his smile.
I hope I was just seeking love.
I hope I smiled back.

AGI and UBI

My son advises me
to spend every penny
we got as one day
soon we'll either be
guerilla fighters living
in a cave and fighting
the AGI's machines,
so money won't
be worth shit,
or we'll be living
off UBI anyway.
I ask him if I can
save a little in case
UBI isn't enough
to go to the movies.

At what point

do the six large
Military Discount
banners at the
Dog Patch Valvoline
become not for
the benefit
of the military but
for the good of the
advertising campaign
directed to the vast
majority of us not
in the armed forces
and who support the
brutal murder of young
men in uniform
by other young men
in uniform? Though
now it's not only
young men,
but women, trans,
and others as well.

Drag or Cross-Dress?

The average human is nineteen
inches wide and eleven inches deep,
for a total circumference of sixty inches,
or five feet, and the hand-embroidered
sari I bought from the embroiderer in a
remote village in the Punjab is twenty-five
feet when laid out, long enough to wrap
five times around an average person.
I was hoping to wear the sari to Hilda
and Jesse, a local restaurant offering
free pancakes to people dressed in drag,
but first I asked a server named Evan
what the difference was between drag
and cross-dressing, wanting to be sure
I qualified for the pancakes, and Evan
gave a scholarly explanation. Drag is a
subset of cross-dressing that involves
a heavy degree of storytelling, that is,
using dress and accessories to create a
character that has their own story.
And cross-dressing, that is, dressing
across genders, is not a simple and
innocuous use of another gender's
sartorial clichés, but in our cultural
moment, is commonly a demeaning
and misogynistic expression of the
male patriarch intentionally weakening
himself by dressing in the clothes
of the subjugated woman and receiving

some perverse pleasure as a result.
Evan said all this and more while
serving a deep green glistening
nettle soup. I have been stung by
nettles many times but simmered
here at Hilda & Jesse's they were
sweet and delicious. Perhaps I
should pay for my pancakes,
I thought, after listening to Evan.
And cross-dressing is not drag so I
might not qualify anyway. It took
me an hour's worth of work time
to accumulate the money to buy
the sari. Thank god I didn't negotiate.
And it took the embroiderer three
months to make it. That's not
including the time for spinning
and dyeing the embroidery thread,
and spinning, dyeing, and weaving
the sumptuous deep blue silk
I imagined my skin wrapped in.
The embroidery was red, yellow,
and green, a jungle scene, trees,
flowers, and birds. I better give
my sari to my female partner
and hope she will let me
unwrap her, slowly,
round and round, like a spiral,
a spiral twisting from the center

of the universe, and then we can
fold it over once and lay down
on it, hopefully forgetting
all our stories. As far as this
story goes, I am reluctant, even
ashamed to tell this to my
children, for gender is a thing
of the past for them. And for them
all clothes are for everyone.
And though they are revolutionaries
they love to dress to the nines.
And as far as my own tired gender
goes, which my children laugh at,
can my angry man be simmered
away and sweetened like the nettles?
I'll ask Evan if they can do that.

x

The Twelve Commandments of Peaceful Nations

1
Immigration is the essence of democracy. Earthlings are free to roam the earth, except for nature preserves.

2
How do the billion people living in prosperous democracies stop the billions living in impoverished tyrannies from over-running their countries? Obviously, by peacefully helping these impoverished tyrannies turn into prosperous democracies and thereby righting the natural flows of immigration.

3
To each according to their needs for shelter, food, education, midwifery services, and sketch pads. All in a place of equality and freedom.

4
When a great teacher retires, every flag in the world should fly at half-mast. There shall be no other half-masts permitted.

5
May every pilot wear a pink tutu, with or without epaulettes.

6
May everyone be a limousine (or at least electric sedan) liberal and a conservative. Liberal = free. Conservative = conserving the natural world.

7
All museum collections shall be disbanded and rotated/distributed among the world's population, without subtraction for fees.

8
All monarchies shall voluntarily disband and their assets distributed to the world's population, without subtraction for fees.

9
Just as the Kurds fill every senior political position with a woman and a man and make sure all ethnic groups are represented, so shall all nations do this.

10
May everyone have a tramp stamp.

11
May everyone dance even if they can't dance.

12
When our law enforcement officers wear black masks and uniforms with no identification, may everyone in the country wear the same, so no one knows who is who.

The Great International No Secrets Agreement

On March 8, 2025, in Kyzyl, Tuva, at the first offsite UN General Assembly, all governments in the world attended and agreed to never again conduct any meetings in secret, including military meetings, political meetings, meetings with citizens, and meetings with other governments and nongovernmental entities. Everything is to be recorded and searchably archived. All representatives also attended the annual Tuvan throat music competition and went home with a gift of a Tuvan ceremonial drum as a memento and to be beaten in their homelands to celebrate this great advance in humanity.

Assholes

are essential
and beautiful, especially
when clean, but not
Elon Asshole, Tim Asshole,
Jeff Asshole, and Mark Asshole,
all coughing up seven figures
to the inauguration,
thinking they're oh so clever.
At least they all have the same
last name, the first step towards
radical equality for all.

Il Duce

recently quoted my saying
*People laugh in dictatorships
and cry in democracies,* as a
literati's defense of his benevolent,
self-sacrificing leadership. I cringed
because I had said it before his
ascension and didn't mean it as
any kind of defense. I meant only life
goes on, that people can cry in the
best of times and laugh on their
way to the gallows, though I am
sure I could not. All I can do is
cringe and try to shut up now,
and pray I won't be quoted again.

Point and Clench

Three men fill a sidewalk form
with concrete on Market Street.
One, the driver in the cement
truck, but not visible in the cab.
And so my first criminal act,
assuming he is a man.
The second has his right hand
lightly on the chute that hangs
off the rotating cement chamber,
his left hand is up and pointing
or clenching in view of the
driver's sideview mirror.
Point and clench. Point means
move the truck up two feet
because a part of the form
has filled and clench means
stop in front of the next empty
section. Point and clench,
but once the driver must
have been looking away
or was day dreaming,
because he didn't, at first,
inch forward, and cascading
mud almost overwhelmed
the quickly filling form.
The point man is nearly
Caucasian, tall with dark
glasses on this foggy
day, so the windows

to his soul are closed.
The third, less Caucasian
and short, wields a flat-edged
shovel with wild strength,
spreading the number six
mud evenly through the form,
chop chop to flatten the mound,
shovel shovel to move the excess
along the narrow channel,
narrow because it's for the curb.
The sound of the shovel moving
through the mud is the sound
of a biped walking quickly
across a gravely beach,
crunch, crunch, crunch,
fast, heavy breathing.
The problem with our
civilization is the three
men (my second crime the
same as the first), can switch
places but they don't. They
can all drive, point and clench,
and shovel like mad,
but they never switch places.

But Not Heavy

Heavyset but
not heavy
older but
not old man
slips out a gated
doorway and
walks awkwardly
but not with a limp
by a bougainvillea wall,
red, night, so the red
is more dried blood
than fresh blood,
and he goes to a car whose
lights flash before he
gets in. He must be
a magician, a kind one,
he is in a bow-tied
tuxedo, on his way to
a fundraising dinner
in support of dismantling
all national borders,
armies, and hierarchies
and diverting the freed
money to food, shelter,
science, art, and
environmental preservation
and restoration,
all the great
conservative causes.

What a pleasure to
dress finely when
saving the world.
May they succeed!
The only thing I can do
to help is paint a picture
of the man, the person,
the creature, hobbling
past the bougainvillea.
May he not have traffic!
I imagine his bowtie
was not prefabricated
and he hand tied it,
not in front of a mirror,
for it is a bit rakish.
That is a-tilt.

Das Kapital

The fleet of gleaming trucks
wasn't just for the customer
to justify paying the inflated
bill with gratitude, but for
the employees as well, so
they wouldn't get any ideas
about quitting and starting
their own electrical company,
because they'd never
accumulate enough capital
for those trucks, not realizing
they could wire a huge
tower coming to and fro
in a secondhand VW Bug.

Great Table

Fresh breads, meats, salads, bespoke
sauce, and everyone going around
the table lamenting the rise of fascism,
story after story, and then I was asked
why I was so quiet. Did I detect,
underneath the question, a fear
that perhaps I was on the wrong
side and not simply too horrified
to talk? Was it my religion or
former occupation, both a little
different than the other atheist
artists in the room?

Two Parents' Views of Hypocritical Socialism

Your example
of your child's
hypocritical
socialism
is that they eat
peppermint
patties.
My example
of my child's
hypocrisy
is that he flies
around the
world at will.
But both
children are
socialist
saints with
no hypocrisy
at all. In fact
they both
walk barefoot,
even in winter.

I Can't Say Where

Somewhere, I can't say where,
there is a giant agave, larger
than any others that have ever
lived, and there is a small village
next to it. It's as large as
a city building. The people in
the village worship this agave
and believe it is the center
of all things and no one from
the outside has ever come
across this plant or village
except for me. I hid and
looked and then left unseen.
I saw a child sliding down
the curve of a rosette,
well away from the barbs.
I believe the plant is simply
the largest and nothing else,
but I won't tell anyone where
it is and beware if you ask.

Days Inn

Let's say you're an upper midlevel
architect in the Days Inn planning
department and private equity has
just injected $3,000,000,000, which,
along with debt, will allow for the
construction of 10,000 new locations,
40% in the US, 60% around the world,
and you have been given the lead to
design the base model that will, in
two years, be recognizable to most
of the world's population, and one
night, when you can't sleep, you think
about pools, and the next morning
you ask the in-house actuary who
advises on the in-house risk
management program, what is the
likelihood of someone drowning
at one of the 10,000 new pools
over the course of a year and after
two days she (the actuary) concludes,
one to two deaths a year, and adds
an asterisk for the impact on the
bottom line related to litigation
resulting from the two deaths, and you
don't ask the more difficult questions,
of the likelihood of death if no pools
and the guests are forced to do
other things for entertainment, say,
go to shooting ranges or high elevation

tightrope walking concessions, but
your gut tells you that number or
likelihood is far less than the two
deaths, so the difference between
one to two, less the other number,
is significant, even just one is, of course,
significant when it comes to death,
as the proverb says *to save one person
is to save the world,* so you leave
the pool out of the plans, not wanting
to be a murderer, though acknowledging
the off-premises deaths wouldn't
effect the bottom line and you know
the design review committee will
ask about pools and make a decision
barely accounting for your insomniac
wisdom, but more related to space,
construction costs, labor, and
comparative revenue projections.

X

Peeled Orange

When my mother
brushed my hair
I was close enough
to her fingers
to smell the orange
she had just peeled.
I thought she was old
but she wasn't.
Tanginess of peel
mixed with sweetness
of flesh. She was
skilled at getting
the orange skin
off, if not in
one piece,
nearly so,
and quickly,
and she could talk
of other things
during the magic.
I have no memory
of her praising
herself for her
peeling skill.
She saved her
praise for the
fruit of the earth.

Man in Black

Some Jews throw a couple shovels
of dirt on the casket, to show, symbolically,
dust to dust, or, dirt to dirt, and then walk away,
but I looked back and saw a man in black,
solitary, shoveling the deep grave full.
I brought my sons back and we took
the extra shovels and pitched in. We were
strong and trying to impress each other,
so it didn't take long, a pity we weren't
weaker and we didn't pause often, so it took
all night and we could walk away
at dawn, a time of day my mother
appreciated, how the light caught
in all the nets of her flowers.

Gentle Giant

You have, in your mind, awkward
dietary restrictions and when you and
your lover conferred at restaurants, then
ordered, he jumped in and told the order
taker he had the dietary restrictions and
placed your special order as if it were
his own, leaving you to remember his
and make that order as if it were yours.
You think because he was a giant and
you are tiny, people should see through
the ruse, the small one ordering
large and the large one ordering small,
but they never did, they only sensed
his kindness, as everyone easily did,
and now that he is suddenly and
tragically gone, it's up to you to tell
the stories so at least his kindness
still makes the rounds. I see you two
across the booth, handing your plates
to each other, like diplomats
exchanging papers, smiling, before
you chow down.

Duned Up

It's not the sands of time but merely
four feet of snow duned up by a few
days' winds and covering all of an old
Harley except for an inch of chrome
handlebar and the well gripped
handle and the leather tassel,
dare I say, tickling the snow;
no, the tassel does not tickle
and the snow is not ticklish.
But I would like to ask the creator
why we don't have two hearts,
one for pumping blood and one
for loving, as we have two eyes,
two hands, two lungs. The loving
heart and the pumping heart
could be cross-trained to do each other's
work so if there was ever a problem
with one or the other they could
take over for each other and even do
both jobs at once, at least temporarily.

Maw

When I eat an animal
or for that matter a plant
I think of the creature
as it was alive and at
the moment of death
by human hands.
I think of the creature
to varying depths
and degrees, or not
at all, as today,
when I ate three small
slices of braised
amberjack maw.
I dreamed of the maw,
the buoyancy bladder,
squeezing closed in the
glistening amberjack,
air bubbling out
as the fish dropped
into the depths, while
the waiter told us what
a maw was. An amberjack
died for us to learn
that word and we don't
know if its maw was
filling or collapsing
when it died for us.

An Elder

How with every chai he said
good or *excellent*
but we caught him once,
when we made the chai
with spoiled camel's milk
so it was too sour to drink
and he said *good, very good*
and when we laughed and
called him out on it
he waved his hand as if
he was bating a fly and said
*it's always good to say
"good" to the one waking
early to prepare my chai.*
His classic humility, but what
he really meant was *it's
always good to say "good,"
no matter what.* And though
he has trouble bending
I saw him bend to pick up
one freshly fallen blossom
and put it on top of the gate.
He watched the breeze
knock it away even before
all the petals relaxed onto
the metal.

Blessings

Subject to minor variations such as
ear size and shape I'm sure
all people look pretty much alike,
though I only want to engage
intimately with a few of them,
subject to some deeply cultural
and personal guidelines; but my
friend Ashwani, walking us through
the Rajput and Brahmin sections
of Jodhpur can easily distinguish
between the two castes and not
just because of a real estate code
set by some petty tyrant who
played polo with the British
less than a century ago.
The Brahmins and Rajputs
looked alike to me,
but once we were safely
in the Brahmin section we
stopped to talk to many of
Ashwani's "uncles," some with
direct genetic associations and
others more vaguely connected.
With every elder uncle Ashhwani
greeted them by touching
their toes with his right big
fingers and then touching his
forehead. A gesture of respect
and a request for a blessing

all in one. I don't remember
any uncles placing hands on
Ashwani's head and mumbling.
There was only lively conversation
which was itself a blessing.
And back at Ashwani's house
he encouraged both his young
children to touch my toes
and then their foreheads
and also to do the same with
my son, not much older than
they were and they
performed the ritual
but with some reluctance
and nervous smiles which
may have denoted their
general unease with the custom
or simply that they regarded us
not as respected elders but
goofy playful cousins from the
other side of the world. They
did it twice though because
Ashwani demanded a second
try after they only made it
to our ankles on the first
and I who never believed in
prayers or blessings or castes
placed my palm briefly
on their heads and felt

blissful, tranquil, positive
thoughts about the
children's futures.
I liked the toe to forehead
greeting and hereby
urge people to replace
the handshake with it. And not
just for elders but with everyone
and anyone.

Baby Taj

Because I am a sadist and I overheard
a tour guide, in Italian-accented Spanish,
describe the four holy rivers of life,
I asked my son if he knew the four holy
rivers of life, and he didn't answer
but asked if I was asking as a teacher
or if I wanted to know the answer
and my answer was a little bit of both
and he said that's the hallmark of
a great teacher and a great student,
not saying which of us was which,
and the guard asked him if he had
any computers, bombs, or dresses
in his bag, laughing at the last question
and winking to her partner. I missed
it all, trying to remember the four
rivers in three languages, but she
was making fun of my son for his long
flowing red hair, no others were
similar here, and I wanted to tell
her he is a holy man and she shouldn't
laugh but revere, and I wanted
to tell my son, you are holy, and life
might get complicated sometimes
because of it, but don't despair,
even if you have to tie your hair
back once in a while or fold it
into your brown cap. And by the way,
the answer, in the language called

English, is water, wine, milk, and honey.
May we all be able to walk unimpeded
to these four rivers with clean jars.

Guru

My son handstitched a book for
my birthday. I didn't know
books are stitched like shirts,
and the artistry of the stitch
is most important, though
it's mostly hidden away.
While working he said to me
*Today I will not choose a guru
from other gurus.* And though
a child may steal from his parents,
never the reverse, I now say,
as if I were the first to say it,
*Never choose a guru from among
gurus.* The first one I said this to
was his older brother who goes
from guru to guru, like restaurants.
Learn from others all you'd like,
I told him, but the only guru
there is in the world is in your
own heart; meet her there.

Ithaca

Young couple getting lost on
the way to the gorge, one says
this way babe the other says
no this way babe both with
tension and I told them the word
babe is one of the few that
should never be used with irony,
just the care, love, and desire
it was invented for and I
prayed this changed their lives,
but I couldn't give them
the directions they stopped
to ask me for, I was just a passing
stranger. I hope my gnarled
staff and the heavy cloak I was
wearing despite it being a scorcher
made them remember my advice.

Cocktail

It said it all, you said it all,
at the authentic dive bar
full of divers, diverticulitis,
and general diversionary
antiques, when you asked
the barkeep for a *cocktail*.
Everyone else in the world
orders a particular cocktail,
a mojito or a moscow mule
or even a martini.
In fact, no one in the 8,000
year history of fermentation,
has ever ordered a *cocktail*.
You did it to take pride
in your ignorance,
your learning, and the great
half-guilty, half-innocent
joy of saying something
that had never been said,
and then when you were
staring at the crimson
amalgam cradled in the
heavy glass blown near Beijing
with Murano influences,
negroni-like, the barkeep's
choice, you realized
nothing ever said had ever
been said before, staring
without drinking, mostly

without drinking, at the
mysterious crimson.
For the lucky ones,
the great buzz of one sip
is more than enough.

Two Fifties

There are three kinds of brothers.
The first ignore each other.
The second dream of living next door
to each other and sharing meals a
couple times a week and the
third want to kill each other.
But there are only two kinds
of sisters. The first, indifferent.
The second, living next door.
Which is why there should
only be women governing
and in all nongovernmental
leadership roles for the next
fifty years, except for leaders
of silent meditation retreats
with fifty participants or less,
where the leader has vowed
silence; a man can still take
that job, as long as he
is good at silence.

A Dear Friend

I have a dear friend,
a genius, Ph.D.
from the best university,
and his life work is to learn
to look the other in the eye
with the most loving tender
curiosity possible, and after
years of effort I'm not sure
he can do this even as well
as the average person
and as his dear friend I don't
know if I should make this
observation to him or let him
simply keep trying as hard
as he can.

Chunky

is the wrong word
but I can't help myself so
I call the skateboarder's great
supple solidity *chunky*.
We watched him speed his skateboard
to the edge of an at least two-foot drop
made up of three steps before
a granite landing, where
the goal was to stick to the
board after spinning it in the air
above the steps and land on it
with arms out, and after the first ten
awkward failures all from the
considerable height, he did
perfect shoulder rolls on the crash,
making the granite seem
of little consequence, and on his
11th attempt, he came very close,
almost sticking it before he hopped
off his board without falling.
We thought he was breaking through
but the next ten attempts after that
were even worse and the crash landings
no longer had graceful shoulder rolls
but awkward crumplings.
Though he still sprang up without
any visible bruises or wincing,
like an expert winter swimmer
who can stay in frigid water

with no expression at all. I wanted
to impart some wisdom to the young
curly-haired man but I couldn't
think of any, other than go home
already before you break a leg.
But clearly he had mastered the art
of falling, the greatest art of all.

Schadenfreude

is to take pleasure
in the misfortune of others.
It's despicable but I wasn't
despicable when I laughed after
the ailing old conductor, by accident,
let the baton fly out of his hand
and graze the ninth first violin's
shoulder before it clattered to the floor,
and after she returned it,
she laughed a little. I laughed
with joy, and I cried,
laughed and cried when the
tenor started his solo in the
third movement. The Schiller poem,
paired with the symphony,
was a protest against the
Hapsburg monarchy and a call
for freedom, but the line I quote
is *even the lowly worm experiences
pleasure.* Indeed, once I
laughed and cried when my son
sang a mandarin pop song about
love, and I was ashamed he thought
I was laughing at him when I was really
just laughing and crying with joy.
At the symphony a five-year-old
boy was next to me and I remembered
when my parents took me to see
B's ninth as a five-year-old.

There are not too many people
alive who have a memory of that night,
as the average age was substantial.
Of course, I always want more
so I hoped the conductor would
lose his baton a second time.
But it didn't happen, though the whole
orchestra did laugh between the second
and third movements when the first violin
said something only they could hear.
We all heard the laughter.
I also never saw that before. And when
we were on the cross-town bus,
after, I could tell by their auras
the people on the bus who were
at the symphony with us,
and we talked and laughed about
the baton and the general magic.
They said *goodbye* when they
got off at their stops but I said
see you. It's my optimism.
I sound foolish but it makes
me laugh and cry to say
see you instead of *bye.*

Erhu

I slipped into the Jackson Street
music shop when the proprietor
was closing the steel accordion gate.
I was looking for an Erhu, the two-
stringed Chinese instrument that
weeps and wails when played expertly,
and they had a row of teak and inlaid
snakeskin beauties for 199 each.
Ken, the proprietor Alan's father,
93, tried to show me how to play
a scale, in Mandarin, manhandling
my fingers, which wouldn't cooperate.
He wouldn't stop teaching and I felt
guilty as his son Alan wanted to close up
and go home. So I said I was tired.
Alan wouldn't accept money
for the lesson. I'm sure their names
aren't Alan and Ken. Chinese people
do that with dumb Americans
who can't even learn a simple scale,
they make their names easier.
Alan was glowing to see his father
happily teaching so I shouldn't have
felt guilty, but been more attentive,
and I did feel guilty when my love
said I should have slipped some
money under the door for the lesson.
I didn't think of that.

Two Bills

I gave Bill $4,500 cash to hold
and give to Raul when he was
halfway through his drywall
soundproof job and Bill said
don't worry Raul is the best
and super trustworthy so he
can give the money right
away. That's the first Bill,
and then, two days later he
asked, with my permission,
if he could take two buses
and a long walk, to see the
status of the demolition phase
and feel Raul out for just what
he was going to do next—that's
the second Bill, and I imagine
Bill in his ironed white oxford
button-down shirt, dashing,
waving a palm as he talked,
full of curiosity and warmth.
It was my partner who said Bill
might be inclined to help,
and I was upset at her for using
the word *might* because Bill
is not a *might* person, he is
mightier than that, he is all that
and he climbs mountains even
though he lives in the city,
and once, in the mountains,

we passed someone I knew and
I imparted some mildly caddy
gossip about this person to Bill
and I could see he was surprised
but he didn't seem to judge me
at all, that's Bill. Both Bills.

Howl's End

If I died tonight the last thing
I told my sons would be about
the seven drafts we have of
the last stanza of Howl.
The first draft, handwritten
with transcription, is of cum
dripping from cock, cock
in mouth and cock hanging
between legs and other
beautiful cock talk that all
vanishes by draft seven,
which replaces the hanging
or standing cock with angels
and spirits and joy and the
lesson for my sons is beware
the perils of revision, it
could just as easily (or even
likely) make matters worse.

Ginsberg, even fifty years ago
would have known it's best
not to question the gender
or sexuality of others, and
his first instinct, to celebrate
the cock, or, most likely,
his own cock, was the way
to go and he should have
stopped there. And I wonder,
today, in the MOMA crown-

jewel Kathy and Richard S.
Fuld Jr. Room why there are
no depictions of sex acts,
or even scenes suggestive
of sex. Does the prohibition
against pornography extend
to all depictions of sex?
Is sex not a part of life and
the lives and emotions
depicted in the masterworks?

Still I love the big group of
happy old ladies twittering
in front of the Jackson Pollock
(number something).
It's not that their CIS
male partners don't
like art, or, I should
say, didn't like art,
it's that none of them
are here anymore
because they ate
too many double
cheeseburgers and
didn't know how to
handle the stress
of work and life
while the women did.

You are probably afraid
of my next question,
which is why the museum
would permit Kathy
to subjugate herself
by yielding her surname
to the Fuld clan and
thereby becoming
their chattel property
in our capitalist patriarchy?
Don't worry, I won't
ask that question
and I don't care about
the answer. But I will
ask why, or at least
lament, that Richard
has included his middle
initial "S" and Kathy
has done no such thing
with her middle name.
Let's let Richard's "S"
die on the vine without
anyone eating the poisoned
fruit of what it stands for.
But let me tell you about
Kathy's "S," which is
really a "W" and short for
Winifred, her great
grandmother, a Rohingya

who fled Buddhist
persecution two turns
of centuries ago, only
to be shipwrecked off
Nova Scotia and one of
three survivors pulled
out of the cauldron
by the crew of a
small fishing dory,
and then on to be
one of the first
women to graduate
from NYU Law School,
and she sketched her
whole life but never
chose to share her work,
unlike Pole Lock or
Pea Casa So who both
chose to enter the
chattel system, enter
their work, that is,
not their bodies.
Winifred was not
her great grandmother's
original name, that's lost,
but I love to include
her story as I am, like
everyone else in the world,
obsessed with the names of the lost.

And I also dedicate myself to
eradicating the names of
the artists and patrons
in the great room of that
great museum, though these
words might be counter productive
to that noble effort. Perhaps
noble silence would have
done that trick, though there
has never been anything noble
about silence and there
never will be.

Pablo Picasso

Will the real Pablo Picasso
please sit down! I am afraid
he is tired. There are at
least three Pablos claiming
to be the real Picasso.
There is the Pablo portrayed
in the show Pablomatic,
but he's just a misogynistic
cad with no new ideas,
and then there is the Pablo
who orchestrated the banquet
for Rousseau, going to great
lengths to humiliate the man
who painted The Hungry Lion,
that Pablo is just a gross thug.
The real Pablo Picasso carried
his portfolio in a kind of wood-
slat backpack, and four days
running he introduced himself
to us on a side street of Cusco,
Hello I am Pablo Picasso,
and we chatted him up and
didn't buy a thing, as we knew
no one buys from the real ones,
and we were starting long walks
through history so we couldn't
carry any canvases anyway;
but on the fifth day we met Pablo
we were returning from our

sojourn so had no excuse and
had the accumulated guilt of
our four previous conversations,
so we bought a delightful Blue
Period Chinchero street scene.
The buildings leaned into the
street slightly, as if they were
folding over the village like so
much dough, and there were
flowers everywhere. As I said
it was the fifth day when we
stopped for Picasso. The real one.
And on the day after,
the sixth day, which is one day
before the day of rest,
which Pablo never observes,
Pablo greeted us again,
as if he had never seen
us before. That's how it is
with the great ones, they can
never remember ordinary people
for long, especially if the great
one paints all night and sells
his work all day,
not sleeping for years.

Sunday Morning

One minute your guts are
under your skin and the next,
the torturer is unwinding
them onto a spool, as depicted
by Poussin in his Martyrdom
of Saint Erasmus, in the
Vatican Collections. Poussin
is famous for finely painted
hands and excellent perspective.
It's a big spool of guts
and hard to imagine how
they fit inside Erasmus.
I hate when people measure
body parts or bodies to make
a point or frighten us.
The gut is forty-five feet
when straightened
like beauty parlor hair.
I hated Mr. Halpern, our
Sunday school director,
for ruining Sunday mornings.
He told us the six-million
Jews killed in the holocaust,
laid end to end,
would stretch all the way
around the earth, but
at least he didn't say how
far their guts would go if
they were straightened.

To the moon and back?
Don't measure. Halpern!
Never measure the dead
and never measure the dying.

Grant Street

Gold paint
on a large steel
roll-up door,
a beatific man/
woman with giant ears,
the painting
creased by the
horizontal steel
seams and mottled
with rust.
The painting
is rolled up and
out of view all day
when the street
is crowded, it only
comes out at night
when the street
empties, except
for one or two
lonely people
wandering by.
Art is only for
lonely people,
and others who
are not lonely
never understand.
In fact, one can never
understand anything
without loneliness.

Joan as Policewoman Prepares to Sing

The truth is I thought it was excessive,
her elaborate rearranging of music stands,
mic height, chair, brushing hair back,
and her pacing in that small space
in front of the quartet, while the two
violins, viola, and cello waxed (or should I say rosined)
poetic, *just be still and sing already,*
I thought, then she limited her movements
and sang and I immediately understood
her preparatory movements and forgave
her. I had no idea the only words would
be *all is loneliness before me,* and that
simple phrase, with all of Joan as
Policewoman's trilling, would take a
long time to complete, and though I
thought of the great loneliness of a loved
one who died alone, and of my children
being young in this fucked-up world
full of arbitrary borders, I smiled
a large smile and could have laughed
but for the horrified looks of my family
beside me, seeing me smile. I'm afraid
their horror made it even more likely
that I'd laugh. But I didn't laugh.
Thank god. Thank no god.

Immigration Is the Essence of Democracy

Tall, 5'11" man, short blond hair,
piercing blue eyes, even his eyebrows
are manicured. He's in a dark pin-
stripe Brooks Brothers suit, no cuffs,
and tasseled Bruno Magli shoes,
unaware of the murder that was
committed in the same type.
He's leaving Mrs. Bartleby's Burgers
on a short break from Harvard
B school, that his father and his
father's father attended, both of
them also going to Goldman after.
I was distracted and knocked into
the man at the entrance; his
Mont Blanc fountain pen fell
out of his breast pocket with the
impact. I picked it up and tried
to hand it back. He clasped my
wrist and said *Please keep it
and write wherever you can and
whenever you can, Immigration
is the Essence of Democracy,
for that is all ye and we need
to know.*

About the Author

Peter Waldor is the author of twenty-nine books of poetry, including *Who Touches Everything,* which won the National Jewish Book Award for poetry. He is also the author of a book of essays, *Seven Quilts*. His book *Gate Posts With No Gate* is a poetry-art collaboration with a group of visual artists. He was the 2014–2015 Poet Laureate of San Miguel County, Colorado. His poetry has appeared widely in magazines, including *Ploughshares, American Poetry Review, The Colorado Review, Fungi Magazine,* and *Mothering Magazine.* He lives in Ophir, Colorado.

www.ingramcontent.com/pod-product-compliance
Lightning Source LLC
Chambersburg PA
CBHW022015160426
43197CB00007B/436